50 Festive Holiday Cocktails for Celebrations

By: Kelly Johnson

Table of Contents

- Eggnog Martini
- Cranberry Moscow Mule
- Spiced Apple Cider Mimosa
- Pomegranate Bellini
- Gingerbread Martini
- Winter White Cosmopolitan
- Hot Chocolate with Peppermint Schnapps
- Cinnamon Toast Cocktail
- Maple Bourbon Smash
- Champagne Punch
- Coconut Cream Pie Martini
- Festive Sangria
- Peppermint Bark Martini
- Sparkling Citrus Sangria
- Mulled Wine
- Holiday Mojito
- Chocolate Peppermint Martini
- Hot Buttered Rum
- Cranberry Old Fashioned
- Sugar Plum Fairy Cocktail
- Rum Punch
- Sparkling Cranberry Lemonade
- Rosemary Gin Fizz
- Chai White Russian
- Apple Cider Margarita
- Vanilla Bourbon Eggnog
- Berry Sparkler
- Spiked Coffee
- Grapefruit and Rosemary Spritzer
- Nutmeg Sour
- S'mores Martini
- Cranberry Fizz
- Orange Spice Mule
- Blackberry Thyme Fizz
- Chocolate Espresso Martini

- Pineapple Upside Down Cake Cocktail
- Honey Ginger Mule
- Frosty Peach Bellini
- Holiday Pina Colada
- Lemon Thyme Collins
- Maple Cinnamon White Russian
- Pepperberry Gin and Tonic
- Tangerine Basil Smash
- Strawberry Balsamic Sparkler
- Caramel Apple Martini
- Holly Jolly Margarita
- Cinnamon Hot Toddy
- Pineapple Cranberry Sparkler
- Ginger Spice Martini
- Chocolate Orange Martini

Eggnog Martini

Ingredients:

- 2 oz eggnog
- 1 oz vodka
- 1 oz rum
- Ground nutmeg (for garnish)

Instructions:

1. In a shaker filled with ice, combine eggnog, vodka, and rum.
2. Shake gently until chilled.
3. Strain into a chilled martini glass and garnish with a sprinkle of nutmeg.

Cranberry Moscow Mule

Ingredients:

- 2 oz vodka
- 1 oz cranberry juice
- 1/2 oz lime juice
- Ginger beer (to top)
- Fresh cranberries and lime wedge (for garnish)

Instructions:

1. In a copper mug, combine vodka, cranberry juice, and lime juice.
2. Fill the mug with ice and top with ginger beer.
3. Stir gently and garnish with fresh cranberries and a lime wedge.

Spiced Apple Cider Mimosa

Ingredients:

- 3 oz apple cider
- 3 oz sparkling wine (Champagne or Prosecco)
- Cinnamon stick (for garnish)

Instructions:

1. In a champagne flute, pour apple cider.
2. Slowly top with sparkling wine.
3. Garnish with a cinnamon stick.

Pomegranate Bellini

Ingredients:

- 2 oz pomegranate juice
- 4 oz sparkling wine (Champagne or Prosecco)
- Pomegranate seeds (for garnish)

Instructions:

1. In a champagne flute, pour pomegranate juice.
2. Slowly add sparkling wine.
3. Garnish with pomegranate seeds.

Gingerbread Martini

Ingredients:

- 2 oz vodka
- 1 oz gingerbread syrup
- 1 oz heavy cream
- Ground cinnamon and ginger (for garnish)

Instructions:

1. In a shaker filled with ice, combine vodka, gingerbread syrup, and heavy cream.
2. Shake well until chilled.
3. Strain into a martini glass and garnish with a sprinkle of cinnamon and ginger.

Winter White Cosmopolitan

Ingredients:

- 1 1/2 oz vodka
- 1 oz white cranberry juice
- 1/2 oz triple sec
- 1/2 oz lime juice
- Lime wheel (for garnish)

Instructions:

1. In a shaker filled with ice, combine vodka, white cranberry juice, triple sec, and lime juice.
2. Shake well until chilled.
3. Strain into a chilled martini glass and garnish with a lime wheel.

Hot Chocolate with Peppermint Schnapps

Ingredients:

- 1 cup hot chocolate (prepared)
- 1 oz peppermint schnapps
- Whipped cream (for topping)
- Crushed peppermint candy (for garnish)

Instructions:

1. Prepare hot chocolate according to your preference.
2. Stir in peppermint schnapps.
3. Top with whipped cream and sprinkle with crushed peppermint candy.

Cinnamon Toast Cocktail

Ingredients:

- 1 oz cinnamon whiskey
- 1 oz Irish cream liqueur
- 1 oz butterscotch schnapps
- Ground cinnamon (for garnish)

Instructions:

1. In a shaker filled with ice, combine cinnamon whiskey, Irish cream, and butterscotch schnapps.
2. Shake well until chilled.
3. Strain into a glass and garnish with a sprinkle of ground cinnamon.

Maple Bourbon Smash

Ingredients:

- 2 oz bourbon
- 1 oz pure maple syrup
- 1/2 oz fresh lemon juice
- Fresh mint leaves
- Lemon wheel and mint sprig (for garnish)

Instructions:

1. In a shaker, muddle mint leaves with lemon juice and maple syrup.
2. Add bourbon and ice, then shake well.
3. Strain into a glass filled with ice and garnish with a lemon wheel and mint sprig.

Champagne Punch

Ingredients:

- 1 bottle Champagne or sparkling wine
- 2 cups cranberry juice
- 1 cup orange juice
- 1/2 cup brandy
- Fresh cranberries and orange slices (for garnish)

Instructions:

1. In a large punch bowl, combine cranberry juice, orange juice, and brandy.
2. Slowly add Champagne or sparkling wine.
3. Stir gently and garnish with fresh cranberries and orange slices.

Coconut Cream Pie Martini

Ingredients:

- 2 oz coconut cream
- 1 oz vanilla vodka
- 1 oz cream
- Toasted coconut flakes (for garnish)

Instructions:

1. In a shaker filled with ice, combine coconut cream, vanilla vodka, and cream.
2. Shake well until chilled.
3. Strain into a martini glass and garnish with toasted coconut flakes.

Festive Sangria

Ingredients:

- 1 bottle red wine
- 1/2 cup brandy
- 1/4 cup orange liqueur
- 2 cups mixed fruit (apples, oranges, pomegranates)
- 1 cup soda water

Instructions:

1. In a large pitcher, combine red wine, brandy, orange liqueur, and mixed fruit.
2. Let sit in the refrigerator for a few hours to meld flavors.
3. Before serving, add soda water and stir gently.

Peppermint Bark Martini

Ingredients:

- 2 oz vanilla vodka
- 1 oz white chocolate liqueur
- 1 oz peppermint schnapps
- Crushed peppermint candy (for rim and garnish)

Instructions:

1. Rim a martini glass with crushed peppermint candy.
2. In a shaker filled with ice, combine vodka, white chocolate liqueur, and peppermint schnapps.
3. Shake well and strain into the prepared glass, garnishing with additional crushed peppermint.

Sparkling Citrus Sangria

Ingredients:

- 1 bottle sparkling wine
- 1/2 cup vodka
- 1 cup orange juice
- 1 cup grapefruit juice
- Citrus slices (oranges, lemons, limes) for garnish

Instructions:

1. In a pitcher, combine vodka, orange juice, and grapefruit juice.
2. Chill in the refrigerator for about an hour.
3. Just before serving, add sparkling wine and garnish with citrus slices.

Mulled Wine

Ingredients:

- 1 bottle red wine
- 1/4 cup brandy
- 1/4 cup honey or sugar
- 2 cinnamon sticks
- 3 star anise
- 4 cloves
- Slices of orange and lemon

Instructions:

1. In a large pot, combine red wine, brandy, honey or sugar, cinnamon sticks, star anise, cloves, and citrus slices.
2. Heat gently over low heat, avoiding boiling, for about 20-30 minutes.
3. Strain and serve warm in mugs or heatproof glasses.

Holiday Mojito

Ingredients:

- 2 oz white rum
- 1 oz fresh lime juice
- 1 oz simple syrup
- Fresh mint leaves
- Club soda
- Cranberries and lime slices (for garnish)

Instructions:

1. In a glass, muddle mint leaves with lime juice and simple syrup.
2. Fill the glass with ice and add white rum.
3. Top with club soda and garnish with cranberries and lime slices.

Chocolate Peppermint Martini

Ingredients:

- 2 oz vanilla vodka
- 1 oz chocolate liqueur
- 1 oz peppermint schnapps
- Crushed candy canes (for rim and garnish)

Instructions:

1. Rim a martini glass with crushed candy canes.
2. In a shaker filled with ice, combine vodka, chocolate liqueur, and peppermint schnapps.
3. Shake well and strain into the prepared glass, garnishing with additional crushed candy canes.

Hot Buttered Rum

Ingredients:

- 2 oz dark rum
- 1 tbsp butter
- 1 tbsp brown sugar
- 1/2 tsp cinnamon
- 1/4 tsp nutmeg
- Boiling water
- Cinnamon stick (for garnish)

Instructions:

1. In a mug, combine butter, brown sugar, cinnamon, and nutmeg.
2. Add dark rum and fill the mug with boiling water.
3. Stir until the butter is melted and garnish with a cinnamon stick.

Cranberry Old Fashioned

Ingredients:

- 2 oz bourbon
- 1/2 oz cranberry juice
- 1/2 oz simple syrup
- 2 dashes Angostura bitters
- Fresh cranberries and orange twist (for garnish)

Instructions:

1. In a mixing glass, combine bourbon, cranberry juice, simple syrup, and bitters.
2. Add ice and stir until well chilled.
3. Strain into a rocks glass over ice and garnish with fresh cranberries and an orange twist.

Sugar Plum Fairy Cocktail

Ingredients:

- 1 oz vodka
- 1 oz plum liqueur
- 1 oz cranberry juice
- 1/2 oz lemon juice
- Sugared rim (for garnish)

Instructions:

1. Rim a cocktail glass with sugar.
2. In a shaker filled with ice, combine vodka, plum liqueur, cranberry juice, and lemon juice.
3. Shake well and strain into the prepared glass.

Rum Punch

Ingredients:

- 2 oz dark rum
- 2 oz pineapple juice
- 1 oz orange juice
- 1 oz grenadine
- Fresh fruit slices (for garnish)

Instructions:

1. In a shaker filled with ice, combine dark rum, pineapple juice, orange juice, and grenadine.
2. Shake well and strain into a glass filled with ice.
3. Garnish with fresh fruit slices.

Sparkling Cranberry Lemonade

Ingredients:

- 1 cup cranberry juice
- 1/2 cup fresh lemon juice
- 1/4 cup simple syrup
- 2 cups sparkling water
- Lemon slices and cranberries (for garnish)

Instructions:

1. In a pitcher, combine cranberry juice, lemon juice, and simple syrup.
2. Stir well and chill in the refrigerator.
3. Just before serving, add sparkling water and garnish with lemon slices and cranberries.

Rosemary Gin Fizz

Ingredients:

- 2 oz gin
- 1 oz fresh lemon juice
- 1 oz rosemary simple syrup
- Club soda
- Fresh rosemary sprig (for garnish)

Instructions:

1. In a shaker filled with ice, combine gin, lemon juice, and rosemary simple syrup.
2. Shake well and strain into a glass filled with ice.
3. Top with club soda and garnish with a fresh rosemary sprig.

Chai White Russian

Ingredients:

- 2 oz vodka
- 1 oz coffee liqueur
- 1 oz chai tea concentrate
- Heavy cream

Instructions:

1. In a glass filled with ice, combine vodka, coffee liqueur, and chai tea concentrate.
2. Stir gently and top with heavy cream.
3. Serve with a sprinkle of cinnamon or nutmeg, if desired.

Apple Cider Margarita

Ingredients:

- 2 oz tequila
- 1 oz apple cider
- 1 oz fresh lime juice
- 1/2 oz orange liqueur
- Cinnamon sugar (for rim)
- Apple slice (for garnish)

Instructions:

1. Rim a glass with cinnamon sugar.
2. In a shaker filled with ice, combine tequila, apple cider, lime juice, and orange liqueur.
3. Shake well and strain into the prepared glass. Garnish with an apple slice.

Vanilla Bourbon Eggnog

Ingredients:

- 2 oz bourbon
- 1 oz vanilla syrup
- 4 oz eggnog
- Nutmeg (for garnish)

Instructions:

1. In a shaker filled with ice, combine bourbon, vanilla syrup, and eggnog.
2. Shake gently to combine and chill.
3. Strain into a glass and garnish with a sprinkle of nutmeg.

Berry Sparkler

Ingredients:

- 1 oz berry liqueur
- 1 oz vodka
- 1 oz fresh lemon juice
- Sparkling water
- Mixed berries (for garnish)

Instructions:

1. In a glass filled with ice, combine berry liqueur, vodka, and lemon juice.
2. Top with sparkling water and stir gently.
3. Garnish with mixed berries.

Spiked Coffee

Ingredients:

- 1 cup brewed coffee
- 1 oz coffee liqueur
- 1 oz Irish whiskey
- Whipped cream (for topping)

Instructions:

1. In a coffee mug, combine brewed coffee, coffee liqueur, and Irish whiskey.
2. Stir gently to combine.
3. Top with whipped cream and serve hot.

Grapefruit and Rosemary Spritzer

Ingredients:

- 2 oz grapefruit juice
- 1 oz gin
- 1/2 oz rosemary simple syrup
- Club soda
- Fresh rosemary sprig (for garnish)

Instructions:

1. In a glass filled with ice, combine grapefruit juice, gin, and rosemary simple syrup.
2. Stir gently and top with club soda.
3. Garnish with a fresh rosemary sprig.

Nutmeg Sour

Ingredients:

- 2 oz bourbon
- 3/4 oz fresh lemon juice
- 1/2 oz simple syrup
- 1/4 tsp ground nutmeg
- Lemon twist (for garnish)

Instructions:

1. In a shaker filled with ice, combine bourbon, lemon juice, simple syrup, and ground nutmeg.
2. Shake well and strain into a rocks glass.
3. Garnish with a lemon twist.

S'mores Martini

Ingredients:

- 2 oz vanilla vodka
- 1 oz chocolate liqueur
- 1 oz marshmallow fluff
- Graham cracker crumbs (for rim)
- Mini marshmallows (for garnish)

Instructions:

1. Rim a martini glass with graham cracker crumbs.
2. In a shaker filled with ice, combine vanilla vodka, chocolate liqueur, and marshmallow fluff.
3. Shake well and strain into the prepared glass, garnishing with mini marshmallows.

Cranberry Fizz

Ingredients:

- 1 oz cranberry juice
- 1 oz vodka
- 1/2 oz lime juice
- Club soda
- Fresh cranberries and lime wedge (for garnish)

Instructions:

1. In a glass filled with ice, combine cranberry juice, vodka, and lime juice.
2. Top with club soda and stir gently.
3. Garnish with fresh cranberries and a lime wedge.

Orange Spice Mule

Ingredients:

- 2 oz vodka
- 1 oz orange juice
- 1/2 oz ginger syrup
- Ginger beer
- Orange slice and cinnamon stick (for garnish)

Instructions:

1. In a glass filled with ice, combine vodka, orange juice, and ginger syrup.
2. Top with ginger beer and stir gently.
3. Garnish with an orange slice and a cinnamon stick.

Blackberry Thyme Fizz

Ingredients:

- 2 oz gin
- 1 oz blackberry syrup
- 1/2 oz fresh lemon juice
- Club soda
- Fresh blackberries and thyme sprig (for garnish)

Instructions:

1. In a shaker filled with ice, combine gin, blackberry syrup, and lemon juice.
2. Shake well and strain into a glass filled with ice.
3. Top with club soda and garnish with fresh blackberries and a thyme sprig.

Chocolate Espresso Martini

Ingredients:

- 2 oz vodka
- 1 oz chocolate liqueur
- 1 oz fresh espresso
- 1/2 oz simple syrup
- Coffee beans (for garnish)

Instructions:

1. In a shaker filled with ice, combine vodka, chocolate liqueur, espresso, and simple syrup.
2. Shake well and strain into a martini glass.
3. Garnish with coffee beans.

Pineapple Upside Down Cake Cocktail

Ingredients:

- 2 oz vanilla vodka
- 1 oz pineapple juice
- 1/2 oz grenadine
- Whipped cream (for topping)
- Cherry (for garnish)

Instructions:

1. In a shaker filled with ice, combine vanilla vodka and pineapple juice.
2. Shake well and strain into a glass filled with ice.
3. Slowly pour grenadine over the top and let it settle. Top with whipped cream and garnish with a cherry.

Honey Ginger Mule

Ingredients:

- 2 oz vodka
- 1 oz honey ginger syrup
- Ginger beer
- Lime wedge (for garnish)

Instructions:

1. In a glass filled with ice, combine vodka and honey ginger syrup.
2. Top with ginger beer and stir gently.
3. Garnish with a lime wedge.

Frosty Peach Bellini

Ingredients:

- 2 oz peach puree
- 1 oz peach schnapps
- Prosecco
- Fresh peach slice (for garnish)

Instructions:

1. In a glass, combine peach puree and peach schnapps.
2. Top with Prosecco and stir gently.
3. Garnish with a fresh peach slice.

Holiday Pina Colada

Ingredients:

- 2 oz coconut rum
- 1 oz pineapple juice
- 1 oz coconut cream
- Nutmeg (for garnish)

Instructions:

1. In a blender, combine coconut rum, pineapple juice, and coconut cream with ice.
2. Blend until smooth and pour into a glass.
3. Garnish with a sprinkle of nutmeg.

Lemon Thyme Collins

Ingredients:

- 2 oz gin
- 1 oz fresh lemon juice
- 1 oz simple syrup
- Club soda
- Fresh thyme sprig and lemon slice (for garnish)

Instructions:

1. In a shaker filled with ice, combine gin, lemon juice, and simple syrup.
2. Shake well and strain into a glass filled with ice.
3. Top with club soda and garnish with a fresh thyme sprig and lemon slice.

Maple Cinnamon White Russian

Ingredients:

- 2 oz vodka
- 1 oz coffee liqueur
- 1 oz maple syrup
- 2 oz heavy cream
- Cinnamon stick (for garnish)

Instructions:

1. In a glass filled with ice, combine vodka, coffee liqueur, and maple syrup.
2. Stir well to combine.
3. Slowly pour heavy cream over the top and garnish with a cinnamon stick.

Pepperberry Gin and Tonic

Ingredients:

- 2 oz gin
- 4 oz tonic water
- 1/2 oz pepperberry syrup
- Lemon wheel and pepperberries (for garnish)

Instructions:

1. In a glass filled with ice, combine gin and pepperberry syrup.
2. Top with tonic water and stir gently.
3. Garnish with a lemon wheel and a few pepperberries.

Tangerine Basil Smash

Ingredients:

- 2 oz tangerine juice
- 1 oz gin
- 1/2 oz honey syrup
- Fresh basil leaves
- Club soda
- Basil sprig (for garnish)

Instructions:

1. In a shaker, muddle fresh basil leaves with honey syrup.
2. Add tangerine juice and gin, then fill with ice.
3. Shake well and strain into a glass filled with ice. Top with club soda and garnish with a basil sprig.

Strawberry Balsamic Sparkler

Ingredients:

- 2 oz strawberry puree
- 1 oz balsamic vinegar
- 4 oz sparkling wine
- Fresh strawberries (for garnish)

Instructions:

1. In a glass, combine strawberry puree and balsamic vinegar.
2. Top with sparkling wine and stir gently.
3. Garnish with fresh strawberries.

Caramel Apple Martini

Ingredients:

- 2 oz vodka
- 1 oz sour apple liqueur
- 1 oz caramel syrup
- Apple slice (for garnish)

Instructions:

1. In a shaker filled with ice, combine vodka, sour apple liqueur, and caramel syrup.
2. Shake well and strain into a martini glass.
3. Garnish with an apple slice.

Holly Jolly Margarita

Ingredients:

- 2 oz tequila
- 1 oz cranberry juice
- 1 oz fresh lime juice
- 1/2 oz orange liqueur
- Lime wedge and cranberries (for garnish)

Instructions:

1. In a shaker filled with ice, combine tequila, cranberry juice, lime juice, and orange liqueur.
2. Shake well and strain into a glass filled with ice.
3. Garnish with a lime wedge and cranberries.

Cinnamon Hot Toddy

Ingredients:

- 2 oz whiskey
- 1 oz honey
- 1 oz fresh lemon juice
- Hot water
- Cinnamon stick and lemon slice (for garnish)

Instructions:

1. In a heatproof glass, combine whiskey, honey, and lemon juice.
2. Fill with hot water and stir until honey is dissolved.
3. Garnish with a cinnamon stick and lemon slice.

Pineapple Cranberry Sparkler

Ingredients:

- 2 oz pineapple juice
- 2 oz cranberry juice
- 4 oz sparkling water
- Lime wedge and pineapple slice (for garnish)

Instructions:

1. In a glass filled with ice, combine pineapple juice and cranberry juice.
2. Top with sparkling water and stir gently.
3. Garnish with a lime wedge and a pineapple slice.

Ginger Spice Martini

Ingredients:

- 2 oz vodka
- 1 oz ginger liqueur
- 1 oz fresh lime juice
- 1/2 oz simple syrup
- Candied ginger (for garnish)

Instructions:

1. In a shaker filled with ice, combine vodka, ginger liqueur, lime juice, and simple syrup.
2. Shake well and strain into a martini glass.
3. Garnish with a piece of candied ginger.

Chocolate Orange Martini

Ingredients:

- 2 oz chocolate liqueur
- 1 oz vodka
- 1 oz orange liqueur
- Orange twist (for garnish)

Instructions:

1. In a shaker filled with ice, combine chocolate liqueur, vodka, and orange liqueur.
2. Shake well and strain into a martini glass.
3. Garnish with an orange twist.